DAY HIKES IN
A S P E N
C O L O R A D O

by Robert Stone

Photographs by Robert Stone
Published by:
Day Hike Books, Inc.
114 South Hauser Box 865
Red Lodge, MT 59068
Copyright 1996
Library of Congress Catalog Card Number: 95-92664

Distributed by:
ICS Books, Inc.
1370 E. 86th Place
Merrillville, IN 46410
1-800-541-7323
Fax 1-800-336-8334

TABLE OF CONTENTS

About the Hikes 4

Map of the Hikes 6

THE HIKES

1. Linkins Lake 8

2. Independence Ghost Town 10

3. The Roaring Fork Braille Trail 12

4. The Grottos 14

5. Weller Lake 16

Photos 18

6. Ute Trail 20

Photos 22

7. Hunter Creek Trail 24

8. Hunter Valley Trail 26

9. Rio Grande Trail 28

10. Conundrum Creek Trail 30

11. Ashcroft Ghost Town and Castle Creek Trail 32

12. Cathedral Lake 34

13. Maroon Creek Trail 36

14. Maroon Lake Scenic Trail 38

15. Crater Lake 40

16. Maroon-Snowmass Trail 42

Information Sources 45

About the Hikes

Colorado is known for the majestic Rocky Mountains which divide the North American continent. Running north and south, the Colorado Rocky Mountains contain 75 percent of all the land above 10,000 feet in the continental United States, including 1000 peaks rising over 10,000 feet and 53 peaks rising over 14,000 feet. 40 percent of Colorado—over 23 million acres—is public land. 600,000 acres are designated to the state's 11 national parks, while national forests encompass 14 million acres. Colorado also has 37 state parks, 222 wildlife areas, and 25 designated wilderness areas. More than 100 rivers flow through the state, including the headwaters of four major rivers—the Arkansas, Colorado, Platt, and Rio Grande. There are 8000 miles of streams, 2000 lakes and reservoirs, thousands of miles of hiking trails, and hundreds of camp-grounds. The Rocky Mountains are home to bear, moose, elk, deer, antelope, big horn sheep, and mountain goats. Needless to say, outdoor recreation in Colorado is a way of life.

The Day Hikes guide to Aspen, Colorado, focuses on scenic day hikes of various lengths. All of the hikes are in and around Aspen, located 200 miles west of Denver.

Although Aspen is best known as a ski resort town, when the snow melts, this mountain community has an active summer life as well. The city is alive with music, food, wine, and film festivals. The downtown area has a pedestrian walking mall, outdoor eateries, gourmet restaurants, boutiques, galleries, quality shops, and museums. Aspen is graced with restored Victorian homes and distinctive brick and sandstone architecture. This historic 1880s mining town (elevation 7920 feet) sits within the Roaring Fork Valley at the base of the 12,500-foot Independence Pass, linking Aspen to Leadville.

Aspen is surrounded by the White River National Forest,

which contains over 2.2 million acres and six 14,000-foot mountain peaks. Seven wilderness areas are also located within this national forest, including Maroon Bells-Snowmass, Hunter-Frying Pan, and Collegiate Peak. There are over 25 rivers and creeks, 31 lakes, numerous canyons with cascading waters and waterfalls, lush valleys covered in wildflowers, and abandoned ghost towns. Whether fishing, river rafting, kayaking, windsurfing, parasailing, hot air ballooning, rock climbing, horseback riding, bicycling, golfing, or hiking, Aspen offers endless opportunities for outdoor recreation. The more than 200 miles of hiking trails make the hiking in this area superb. My goal is to share some of these hikes with you and others, providing visitors as well as locals easy access to the backcountry.

The major access road to all these hikes is Highway 82, which runs east and west from Independence Pass, through the town of Aspen, and west towards Glenwood Springs. These hikes are detailed on the Trails Illustrated maps and United States Geological Survey topo maps which are listed with each hike and can be purchased at most area sporting goods stores. All of these hikes require easy to moderate effort and are timed at a leisurely rate. If you wish to hike faster or go further, set your own pace accordingly. As I hike, I enjoy looking at clouds, rocks, wildflowers, streams, vistas, and any other subtle pleasures of nature. While this adds to the time, it also adds to the experience.

As for attire and equipment, tennis shoes, as opposed to hiking boots, are fine for any of these hikes. Layered clothing, a rain poncho, hat, sunscreen, mosquito repellent, and drinking water are recommended. Pack a lunch for a picnic at scenic outlooks, streams, or wherever you find the best spot.

Enjoy your hike!

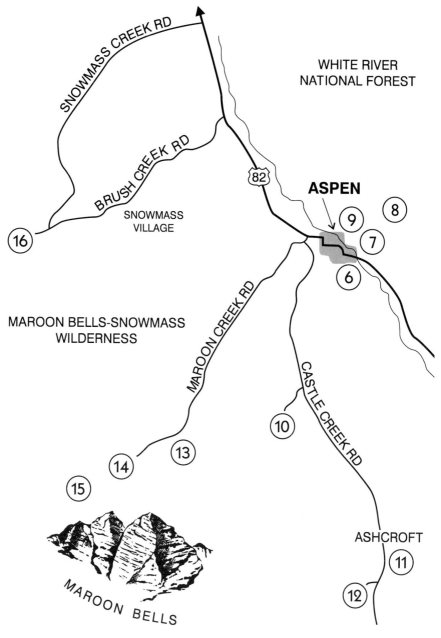

TO BASALT, CARBONDALE & GLENWOOD SPRINGS

SNOWMASS CREEK RD

BRUSH CREEK RD

WHITE RIVER
NATIONAL FOREST

82

ASPEN

⑧

⑨

⑦

⑯

SNOWMASS
VILLAGE

⑥

MAROON CREEK RD

MAROON BELLS-SNOWMASS
WILDERNESS

CASTLE CREEK RD

⑩

⑭

⑬

⑮

ASHCROFT

⑪

⑫

MAROON BELLS

MAP OF

HUNTER-FRYINGPAN
WILDERNESS

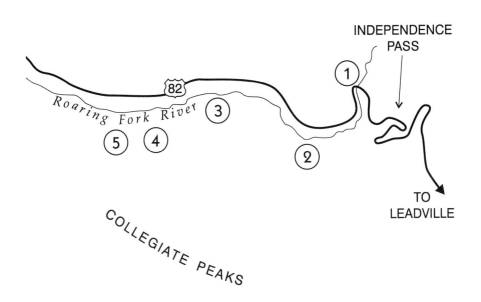

THE HIKES

Hike 1
Linkins Lake

Hiking distance: 1.2 miles round trip
Hiking time: 1.5 hours
Elevation gain: 500 feet
Topo: Trails Illustrated Aspen/Independence Pass
U.S.G.S. Mount Champion and Independence Pass

Summary of hike: Linkins Lake is a high, alpine, glacial lake located near the Continental Divide. The majestic Twining Peak and La Plata Peak loom over an already top-of-the-world location. Throughout the hike are views of the spillway from Linkins Lake as it cascades down to the Roaring Fork River. The headwaters of the Roaring Fork River are located at Independence Lake, less than two miles away.

Driving directions: From downtown Aspen, drive 18 miles east on Highway 82 towards Independence Pass. Just past mile marker 59, the road takes a sweeping curve to the right. Parking pullouts are on both sides of the road along this curve. The trailhead is on the left (north) side of the highway.

Hiking directions: From the parking pullouts, the signed trailhead is to the north. The trail follows a stream on the right. At 0.2 miles is a stream crossing. Across the stream is a posted trail junction. Take the left trail to Linkins Lake. (The trail to the right is the Lost Man Trail and leads to Independence Lake.) Continue 0.4 miles to the lake. After exploring the lake, return along the same trail.

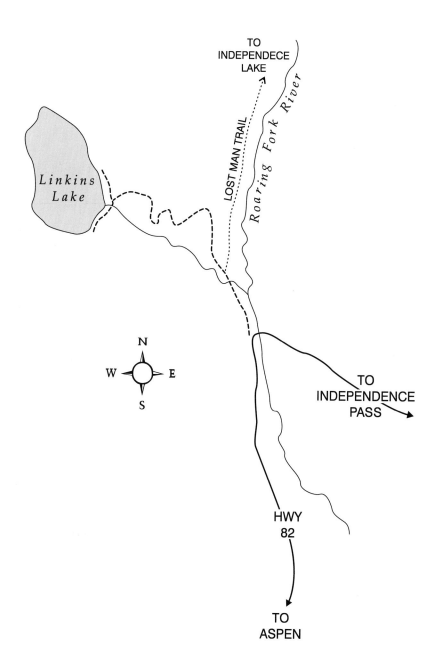

TO
INDEPENDECE
LAKE

Roaring Fork River

LOST MAN TRAIL

Linkins Lake

N
W E
S

TO
INDEPENDENCE
PASS

HWY
82

TO
ASPEN

LINKINS LAKE

Hike 2
Independence Ghost Town

Hiking distance: 1 mile loop
Hiking time: 1 hour
Elevation gain: Level hiking
Topo: Trails Illustrated Aspen/Independence Pass
U.S.G.S. Independence Pass
Aspen Historical Society brochure

Summary of hike: Nestled in the Roaring Fork Valley at 10,920 feet, the town of Independence was founded on the 4th of July in 1879. With the discovery of gold, Independence quickly grew to 1500 residents by 1882. The town included three post offices, three saloons, and four markets. By 1888, the population dwindled to 100 due to a lack of gold and harsh winters. This hike wanders through the town of Independence, where log cabins and mining structures still remain.

Driving directions: From downtown Aspen, drive 16 miles east on Highway 82 towards Independence Pass. The parking turnout is on the right near mile marker 57.

Hiking directions: From the parking turnout, the trail heads south down the steps. The trail to the right leads through the abandoned town. From here, various trails lead to the other structures and ruins. Wander freely among the buildings and surrounding trails. It is easy to see where you are without getting lost.

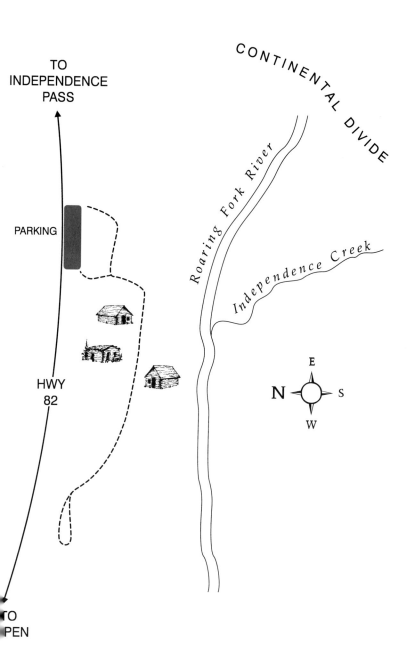

TO
INDEPENDENCE
PASS

CONTINENTAL DIVIDE

Roaring Fork River

Independence Creek

PARKING

HWY
82

E
N ✦ S
W

TO
PEN

INDEPENDENCE
GHOST TOWN

Hike 3
The Roaring Fork
Braille Trail

Hiking distance: 0.25 mile loop
Hiking time: 40 minutes
Elevation gain: Level hiking
Topo: Trails Illustrated Aspen/Independence Pass
U.S.G.S. Thimble Rock and New York Peak

Summary of hike: Established in 1967, the Braille Nature Trail was the first trail of its kind. Located at 10,400 feet, this quarter mile loop is a gentle, soothing meander through the forest. The trail has 22 learning stations and a nylon guide wire to assist the blind to the stations. The text at each station is written in English and Braille and describe the immediate surroundings through touch, smell, and sound. The stations teach about the trees, their bark, leaves, and needles. They teach about the ground cover, the Roaring Fork River, the streams, and wildlife. There are now over sixty Braille Trails in the United States. It is an educational and fun experience for both young and old, for the blind and those with sight.

Driving directions: From downtown Aspen, drive 12.5 miles east on Highway 82 towards Independence Pass to the Braille Trail turnoff on the right. A "Braille Trail" sign is posted on the north side of the highway. Turn right and continue 0.1 miles to the trailhead parking area.

Hiking directions: From the parking area, you will see the trailhead. A 30-foot bridge crosses over the Roaring Fork River. Once over the river, close your eyes and follow the guide wire.

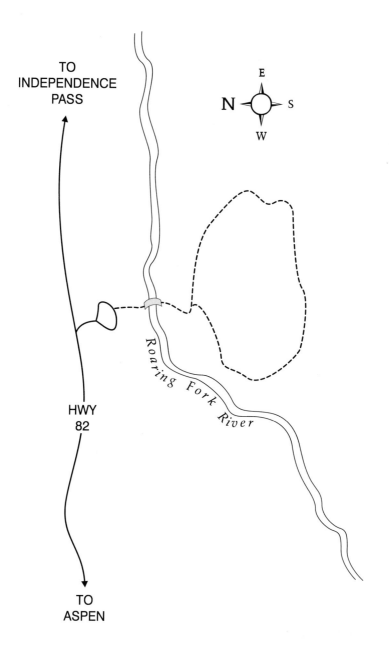

THE ROARING FORK
BRAILLE TRAIL

Hike 4
The Grottos

Hiking distance: 1 mile loop
Hiking time: 1 hour to all day
Elevation gain: 100 feet
Topo: Trails Illustrated Aspen/Independence Pass
U.S.G.S. New York Peak

Summary of hike: This easy hike has it all—waterfalls, pools, ice caves, overlooks, riverfront picnic tables, forests, unusual time-carved rock formations, rock cliffs, and sunbathing rocks. The glacial boulders date back 8000 years. There are wagon tracks from the 1800s etched in the rock, and rocks carved from water and ice, creating small pools. The area is magic. It is a great place to explore for an hour or the whole day.

Driving directions: From downtown Aspen, drive 9 miles east on Highway 82 towards Independence Pass. 0.4 miles past mile marker 50 and 0.9 miles past the Weller Campground, turn right onto an unpaved road. (There is no signage at the turnoff.) The parking area is 200 feet ahead.

Hiking directions: From the parking area, cross the long, wooden footbridge over the Roaring Fork River. Follow the old stage road, which curves to the left. A short distance ahead are many trail options. Posted signs will lead you to the ice caves. The Grottos are easiest and most enjoyable to explore without a formal route. Trails wind through the forest, alongside the river, and to the rock formations. All of the many side trails lead back to the main trail.

There is another set of trails to the right of the parking area. These interconnecting trails loop amongst the rock formations and along the Roaring Fork River. All the trails will eventually bring you back to the trailhead and parking lot.

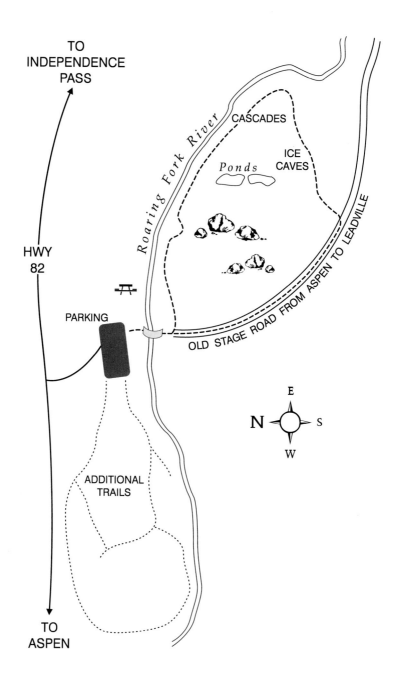

THE GROTTOS

Hike 5
Weller Lake

Hiking distance: 1.2 miles round trip
Hiking time: 1 hour
Elevation gain: 300 feet
Topo: Trails Illustrated Aspen/Independence Pass
          U.S.G.S. New York Peak

Summary of hike: Weller Lake sits in a beautiful bowl below Difficult Peak and New York Peak. This hike follows a forested trail en route to Weller Lake. Along the way is a bridge crossing the Roaring Fork River. There are also several streams tumbling down to meet the river.

Driving directions: From downtown Aspen, drive 8 miles east on Highway 82 towards Independence Pass. The turnoff to the parking area is on the right side of the road 0.5 miles past mile marker 49 and directly across the road from the Weller Campground.

Hiking directions: From the parking area, walk down the steps to a junction. Take the trail to the right, down river, to a wooden bridge crossing the Roaring Fork River. Cross the bridge and take the trail to the right. Several switchbacks will lead you gently uphill. Continue past the stream crossings to a small bridge. A short distance past the bridge is the north shore of Weller Lake. Return along the same trail.

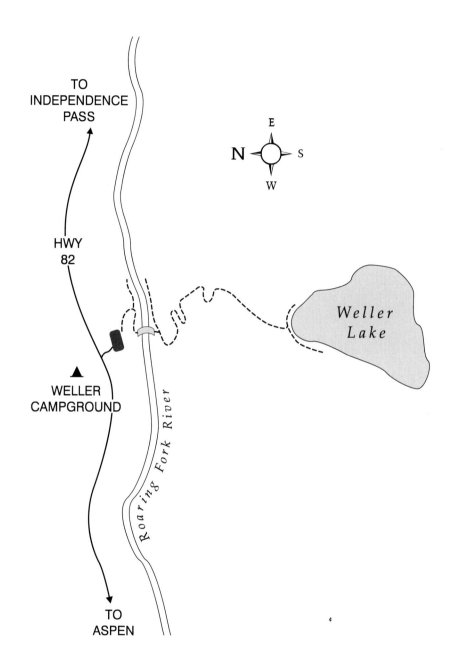

TO
INDEPENDENCE
PASS

HWY
82

WELLER
CAMPGROUND

Weller
Lake

Roaring Fork River

TO
ASPEN

E
N — S
W

WELLER LAKE

Snow in the summer at Linkins Lake - Hike 1

Bridge over the Roaring Fork River at the Braille Trail - Hike 3

Independence Ghost Town - Hike 2

Up the valley on the Conundrum Creek Trail - Hike 10

Hike 6
Ute Trail

Hiking distance: 2 miles round trip
Hiking time: 1.5 hours
Elevation gain: 1200 feet
Topo: Trails Illustrated Aspen/Independence Pass
U.S.G.S. Aspen

Summary of hike: The Ute Trail is a one-mile steady uphill climb to an overhanging rock outcrop. From the top is a commanding view of Aspen and the valley floor. The trail contains eighteen switchbacks while gaining 1200 feet. Tree roots and rocks embedded in the trail aid in secure footing.

Driving directions: From downtown Aspen, walk or drive east to Original Street. Turn right and drive south, towards the mountain, to the end of the road at Ute Avenue. Turn left on Ute Avenue and continue 0.4 miles to the trailhead on the right. A parking area is located on the left.

Hiking directions: From the parking area, cross Ute Avenue to the well-marked trailhead. The trail is a series of switch-backs that begins in the brush and leads through an evergreen and aspen forest. Continue up to the rock outcroppings. From here, many hikers stop and spend time enjoying the grand views of the valley before returning. Take the same route back.

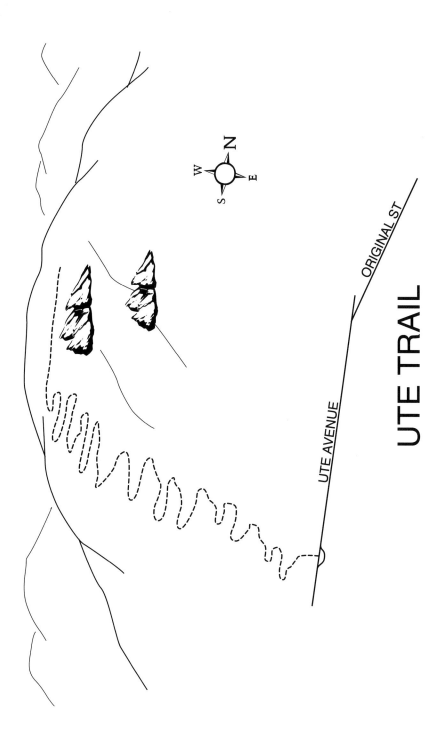

UTE TRAIL

ORIGINAL ST

UTE AVENUE

N
W E
S

A view from the Cathedral Lake Trail - Hike 12

Reservoir Bridge in Hunter Valley - Hike 8

Malamute Peak above the Ashcroft Hotel - Hike 11

The Maroon Bells near Crater Lake - Hike 15

Hike 7
Hunter Creek Trail

Hiking distance: 2 miles round trip
Hiking time: 1.5 hours
Elevation gain: 450 feet
Topo: Trails Illustrated Aspen/Independence Pass
      U.S.G.S. Aspen

Summary of hike: This hike begins in Aspen and follows Hunter Creek upstream. The trail crosses Hunter Creek five times via footbridges. Dense vegetation and the roar of this cascading creek are constant throughout the hike. A waterfall can be viewed from Benedict Bridge.

Driving directions: From the intersection of Main Street and Mill Street in downtown Aspen, drive 0.4 miles north on Mill Street. You will cross the Roaring Fork River bridge. Then bear left on Red Mountain Road to the first road on the right— Lone Pine Road. Turn right and park wherever you find an available space.

Hiking directions: The Hunter Creek trailhead is on the north side of Lone Pine Road. It is located about 100 yards from the intersection of Red Mountain Road and Lone Pine Road, next to the Aspen Community Center. The trail begins with a series of boardwalks, then quickly meets and stays close to the white, tumbling waters of Hunter Creek. It winds through the forest and crosses a succession of bridges over the creek. Just short of one mile, there will be a water spillway in the creek. Hunter Creek Road will be above on the left. A short distance ahead is Benedict Bridge. From the bridge, you will see a waterfall to the left cascading down Red Mountain. Although this trail continues into Hunter Creek Valley, Benedict Bridge is the turnaround spot for this hike. To return, follow the same trail downstream and back to the trailhead.

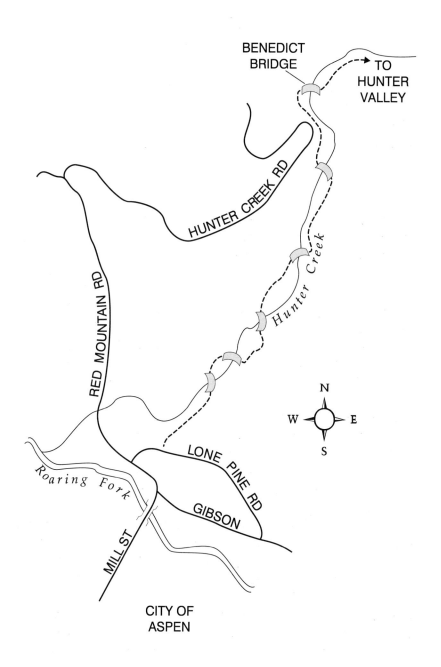

BENEDICT
BRIDGE

TO
HUNTER
VALLEY

HUNTER CREEK RD

Hunter Creek

RED MOUNTAIN RD

N

W   E

S

Roaring Fork

LONE PINE RD

GIBSON

MILL ST

CITY OF
ASPEN

HUNTER CREEK TRAIL

Hike 8
Hunter Valley Trail

Hiking distance: 4 miles round trip
Hiking time: 2 hours
Elevation gain: 400 feet
Topo: Trails Illustrated Aspen/Independence Pass
         U.S.G.S. Aspen

Summary of hike: The Hunter Valley Trail follows Hunter Creek into a beautiful meadow carpeted in wildflowers. Along the way are three bridge crossings over Hunter Creek, abandoned log cabins, and spectacular views of the surrounding mountains.

Driving directions: From Main Street and Mill Street in downtown Aspen, drive north on Mill Street, bear left on Red Mountain Road, and drive to Hunter Creek Road, a total distance of 1.3 miles. Turn right and continue 0.3 miles to the posted Hunter Creek Trailhead road on the left—turn left. The road curves left, then right, then left again to the parking lot at the end of the road.

Hiking directions: From the parking lot, walk back along the road 300 feet to the downhill side of the storage building. The trailhead and posted sign are located here. The trail climbs and curves left before dropping into a forested coulee. At the first junction, take the trail to the right to an asphalt road. Continue 100 feet to the sign posted "Hunter Creek Trail" on the left. The trail crosses Hunter Creek via Benedict Bridge. After crossing the bridge, you can spot a waterfall to the left cascading down Red Mountain. Continue up canyon, paralleling Hunter Creek, to the forest service boundary and trail sign located one mile from the trailhead. The trail then crosses Tenth Mountain Bridge into a pleasant meadow with old log buildings. Continue to Reservoir Bridge, an old log footbridge. Across the bridge is another old log house, dammed spillways, and cold water swimming holes.
    This is our turnaround spot. For those who wish to keep hiking, the trail continues to the Hunter-Frying Pan Wilderness and the Woody Creek Trail. Return by retracing your steps.

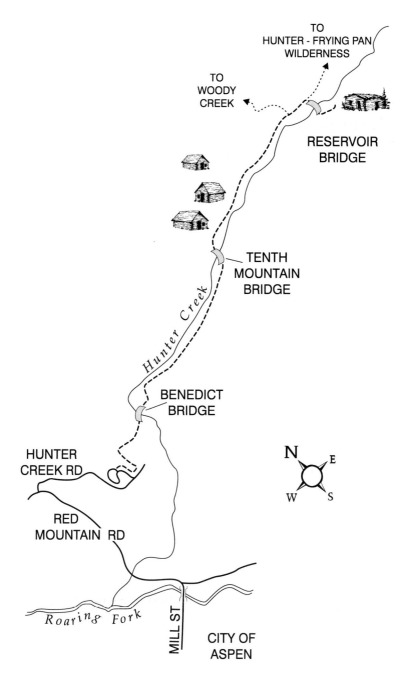

TO
HUNTER - FRYING PAN
WILDERNESS

TO
WOODY
CREEK

RESERVOIR
BRIDGE

TENTH
MOUNTAIN
BRIDGE

Hunter Creek

BENEDICT
BRIDGE

HUNTER
CREEK RD

RED
MOUNTAIN RD

N
E
W
S

Roaring Fork

MILL ST

CITY OF
ASPEN

HUNTER VALLEY TRAIL

Hike 9
Rio Grande Trail

Hiking distance: 4 miles round trip
Hiking time: 2 hours
Elevation gain: Level hiking
Topo: Trails Illustrated Aspen/Independence Pass
U.S.G.S. Aspen

Summary of hike: The Rio Grande Trail begins in Aspen and follows the Roaring Fork River along a paved path. The trail winds through the woods and includes views of beautiful private homes. This path is used by hikers, bikers, and joggers. There are distance markers every quarter mile. Several bridges span the river, and sitting benches are placed along the route.

Driving directions: Walk or drive to downtown Aspen. Park in or near the public parking structure. It is located at North Mill Street and Rio Grande Place, by the visitor center and the post office.

Hiking directions: From the parking structure, cross North Mill Street and walk downhill (north) one block to Puppy Smith Street. Turn left and walk a half block to the marked trail entrance. Take the left trail heading west, crossing a wooden bridge over the Roaring Fork River. This winding trail parallels the river downstream. A short distance past the 1-3/4 mile marker is Slaughterhouse Bridge. Although our turnaround spot is the bridge, the trail continues for several miles, passing the Airport Business Center, towards Woody Creek. To return, retrace your steps.

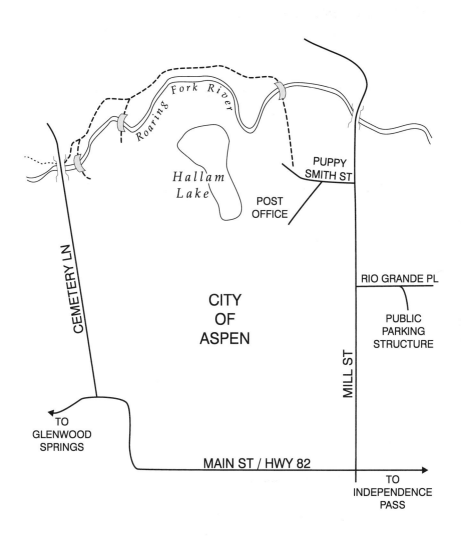

RIO GRANDE TRAIL

Hike 10
Conundrum Creek Trail

Hiking distance: 5 miles round trip
Hiking time: 2.5 hours
Elevation gain: 600 feet
Topo: Trails Illustrated Aspen/Independence Pass
U.S.G.S. Hayden Peak and Maroon Bells

Summary of hike: This hike follows Conundrum Creek up the valley. The trail meanders through open meadows covered in wildflowers and an aspen and lodgepole pine forest. Throughout the hike you will see and hear Conundrum Creek as it makes its way to join Castle Creek downstream. Hayden Peak and Conundrum Peak overlook this valley. In August, wild raspberries can be found along the trail.

Driving directions: From Aspen, drive 0.5 miles west of town on Highway 82 to Maroon Creek Road. Turn left and quickly turn left again on Castle Creek Road (Highway 102) towards Ashcroft. Continue 4.8 miles to Conundrum Creek Road on the right—turn right. Drive 1 mile to the trailhead parking area at the end of the road.

Hiking directions: From the parking area, the trail heads south past the metal gate and trailhead sign. The trail parallels Conundrum Creek, slightly gaining elevation all the way. At 1.7 miles is an old log cabin in a meadow surrounded by aspen trees. At 2.5 miles is the Conundrum Creek log crossing. This is our turnaround spot. Return along the same trail.

Many people continue after crossing Conundrum Creek to two hot spring pools. From the trailhead, it is 8.5 miles one way to the pools, including three creek crossings. The crossings can be dangerous. If you continue, use caution.

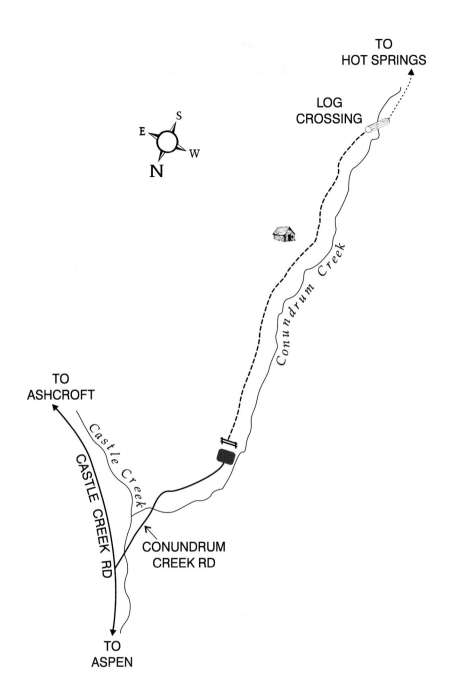

TO
HOT SPRINGS

LOG
CROSSING

Conundrum Creek

S

E

W

N

TO
ASHCROFT

Castle Creek

CASTLE CREEK RD

CONUNDRUM
CREEK RD

TO
ASPEN

CONUNDRUM CREEK TRAIL

Hike 11
Ashcroft Ghost Town and
Castle Creek Trail

Hiking distance: 3 miles round trip
Hiking time: 1.5 hours
Elevation gain: Level hiking
Topo: Trails Illustrated Aspen/Independence Pass
U.S.G.S. Hayden Peak
Aspen Historical Society brochure

Summary of hike: The abandoned mining town of Ashcroft was built in 1880. Originally home to 2500 residents, Ashcroft had twenty saloons and was larger than Aspen. By 1885, the town dwindled to 100 residents due to the low grade ore. Nine original log buildings remain and are maintained.

This hike begins by walking through Ashcroft. It leads to a foot trail that follows Castle Creek upstream through the valley, surrounded by 13,000-foot mountain peaks.

Driving directions: From Aspen, drive 0.5 miles west on Highway 82 to Maroon Creek Road. Turn left and quickly turn left again on Castle Creek Road (Highway 102) towards Ashcroft. Continue 11 miles to the Ashcroft parking lot on the left.

Hiking directions: From the parking lot, walk the boardwalk through Ashcroft. At the south end of town, the boardwalk ends and a foot trail leads into an aspen grove. The foot trail parallels Castle Creek on the left and Castle Creek Road, high above, on the right. At 0.6 miles the trail forks. Follow the left fork, crossing a small wooden bridge by a beaver pond and staying close to the creek. (The right fork leads to the highway.) At 0.9 miles, the trail leads into a meadow above Castle Creek covered in multicolored wildflowers. Past the meadow, the trail ends as it meets Castle Creek Road at the Pine Creek Cookhouse restaurant. To return, retrace your steps.

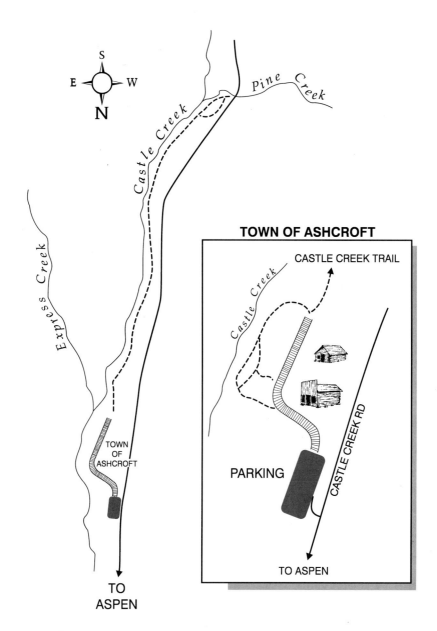

ASHCROFT GHOST TOWN
AND
CASTLE CREEK TRAIL

Hike 12
Cathedral Lake

Hiking distance: 5.5 miles round trip
Hiking time: 3.5 hours
Elevation gain: 1975 feet
Topo: Trails Illustrated Aspen/Independence Pass
U.S.G.S. Hayden Peak

Summary of hike: This hike parallels the white cascades and crashing waterfalls of Pine Creek. The hike ends at the glacial Cathedral Lake. Surrounding this alpine lake are towering rock formations resembling cathedral spires. The lake sits beneath the shadows of Cathedral Peak, standing at 13,943 feet. The elevation gain is nearly 2000 feet. It is a steady uphill climb all the way.

Driving directions: From Aspen, drive 0.5 miles west of town on Highway 82 to Maroon Creek Road. Turn left and quickly turn left again on Castle Creek Road (Highway 102) towards Ashcroft. Continue 12 miles to the Cathedral Lake turnoff on the right. This turnoff is at the 12-mile marker. Turn right and drive 0.6 miles to the parking lot at the end of the road.

Hiking directions: From the parking lot, the trailhead is easy to see and the trail is easy to follow. It is a steady climb through an aspen and evergreen forest. Along the way the trail crosses boulder fields while following the endless tumbling braids of Pine Creek. The final approach to the lake is a steep series of short switchbacks, with dramatic, rugged mountain spires on the right. At the top of the switchbacks is a signed trail junction. Take the left fork a short distance to Cathedral Lake. (The right fork leads two miles to Electric Pass.) Near the lake, the trail crosses Pine Creek and descends to the lake shore. Return along the same trail.

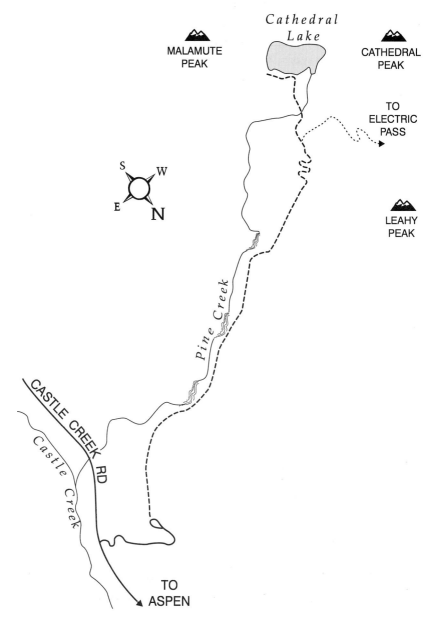

CASTLE PEAK

CONUNDRUM PEAK

Cathedral Lake

MALAMUTE PEAK

CATHEDRAL PEAK

TO ELECTRIC PASS

LEAHY PEAK

Pine Creek

CASTLE CREEK RD

Castle Creek

TO ASPEN

CATHEDRAL LAKE

Hike 13
Maroon Creek Trail

Hiking distance: 3.25 miles one-way (see driving directions)
Hiking time: 1.5 hours
Elevation gain: Downhill 600 feet
Topo: Trails Illustrated Maroon Bells/Redstone/Marble
U.S.G.S. Maroon Bells and Highland Peak

Summary of hike: The Maroon Creek Trail parallels the creek downstream through this magnificent valley formed by rivers of glacial ice. There are continuous cascades, small waterfalls, bridge crossings, boulder fields, and aspen and evergreen forests.

Driving directions: For this hike I highly recommend taking the RFTA Maroon Bells bus from downtown Aspen. The enthusiastic and knowledgeable bus drivers describe the geology of the area along the way. The bus leaves you off at the trailhead and will pick you up alongside the road, returning you to Aspen. The buses return every 20 to 30 minutes. The terminal is located at Rubey Park on Durant Avenue between Mill Street and Galena Street.

Hiking directions: From the trailhead overlooking Maroon Lake, take the trail to the left. This leads to the outlet stream (east end) of Maroon Lake. Follow Maroon Creek downstream to a footbridge. Cross the bridge and continue downstream. You will walk through a boulder field and pass a bridge on the left. Stay on the main trail, which crosses a bridge over East Maroon Creek just before it merges with Maroon Creek. Farther along, you will see picnic benches and another bridge that crosses Maroon Creek—cross the bridge. This is East Maroon Portal. Walk up to Maroon Creek Road. Wait along the roadside and the RFTA bus will pick you up and return you to downtown Aspen.

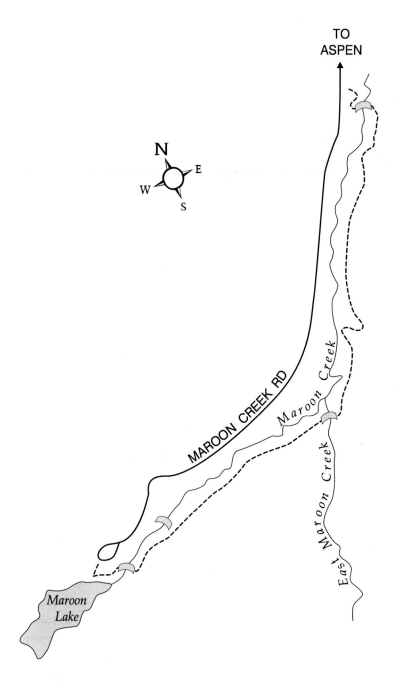

TO
ASPEN

N
W E
S

MAROON CREEK RD

Maroon Creek

East Maroon Creek

Maroon
Lake

MAROON CREEK TRAIL

Hike 14
Maroon Lake Scenic Trail

Hiking distance: 2 mile loop
Hiking time: 1 hour
Elevation gain: 300 feet
Topo: Trails Illustrated Maroon Bells/Redstone/Marble
U.S.G.S. Maroon Bells

Summary of hike: The Maroon Lake Scenic Trail follows the west shore of Maroon Lake in full view of the three towering Maroon Bell Peaks—Pyramid Peak, South Maroon Peak, and North Maroon Peak—rising 4000 feet above the lake (cover photo). The trail includes bridge crossings over Maroon Creek, a beaver pond, and the Maroon Creek waterfall.

Driving directions: Due to the popularity of the Maroon Valley, to help reduce damage to the area, you may only access the area by car before 8:30 a.m. or after 5 p.m. each day. During the rest of the day, a bus shuttle service (RFTA) departs from Rubey Park in Aspen every 20 to 30 minutes from 9 a.m. to 4:30 p.m. daily. Rubey Park is located on Durant Avenue between Mill Street and Galena Street.

If you choose to drive, go 0.5 miles west of Aspen on Highway 82 to Maroon Creek Road. Turn left and continue 9.5 miles to the Maroon Lake parking lots and trailhead.

Hiking directions: From the parking lot, walk to the end of the road to the well-marked trailhead. From here you will have an elevated view of Maroon Lake. Descend the steps and take the trail leading directly towards the north shore of the lake. Continue along the shoreline to a footbridge over Maroon Creek. Cross the creek and head upstream to a second footbridge. From this bridge is a view of a beautiful waterfall. After crossing the bridge, take the left trail upstream. At the far end of the pond is a junction. Take the left branch, circling around the pond back to the bridge and waterfall. Cross the bridge again, and take the right trail back to the trailhead.

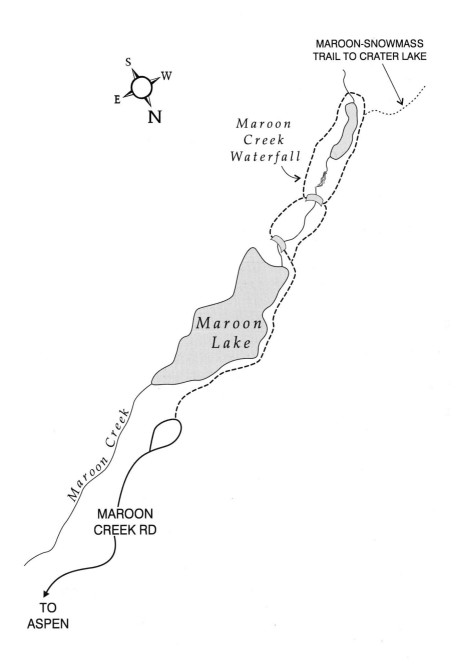

MAROON-SNOWMASS
TRAIL TO CRATER LAKE

Maroon Creek Waterfall

Maroon Lake

Maroon Creek

MAROON CREEK RD

TO ASPEN

S W E N

MAROON LAKE TRAIL

Hike 15
Crater Lake

Hiking distance: 3.6 miles round trip
Hiking time: 2 hours
Elevation gain: 500 feet
Topo: Trails Illustrated Maroon Bells/Redstone/Marble
U.S.G.S. Maroon Bells

Summary of hike: Considered the most photographed mountains in the world, the Maroon Bells were named for their color and bell-like shapes. Crater Lake sits at the base of these imposing 14,000-foot peaks. The trail to Crater Lake is in full view of these peaks. Highlights along the way include beaver ponds, meadows covered in wildflowers, bridge crossings, Maroon Lake, and the Maroon Creek waterfall.

Driving directions: Due to the popularity of the Maroon Valley, to help reduce damage to the area, you may only access the area by car before 8:30 a.m. or after 5 p.m. each day. During the rest of the day, a bus shuttle service (RFTA) departs from Rubey Park in Aspen every 20 to 30 minutes from 9 a.m. to 4:30 p.m. daily. Rubey Park is located on Durant Avenue between Mill Street and Galena Street.
   If you choose to drive, go 0.5 miles west of Aspen on Highway 82 to Maroon Creek Road. Turn left and continue 9.5 miles to the Maroon Lake parking lots and trailhead.

Hiking directions: From the parking lot, walk to the end of the road to the well-marked trailhead overlooking Maroon Lake. Descend the steps and take the trail to the right, along the far end of the meadow from Maroon Lake. The trail leads through an aspen forest and past the head of Maroon Lake to a signed trail junction. Take the right fork, continuing on the Maroon-Snowmass Trail. The trail goes through a boulder field. Before long, you will be looking down on Crater lake. Continue down to the lake. The trail leads around the northwest side of the lake at the base of North Maroon Bell. To return, take the same trail back.

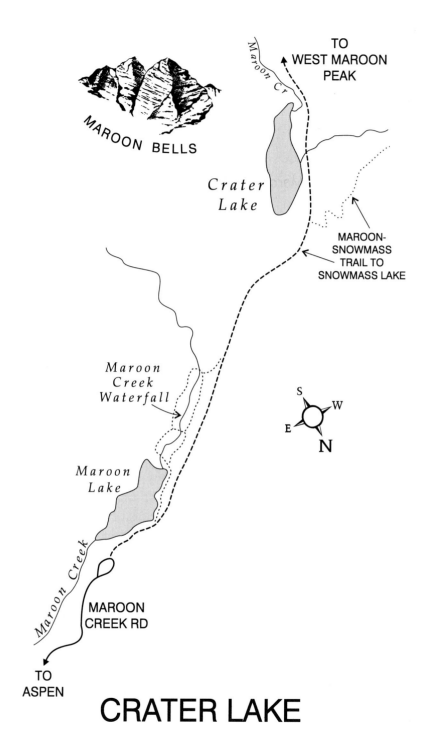

TO
WEST MAROON
PEAK

Maroon Cr

MAROON BELLS

*Crater
Lake*

MAROON-
SNOWMASS
TRAIL TO
SNOWMASS LAKE

*Maroon
Creek
Waterfall*

S
W
E
N

*Maroon
Lake*

Maroon Creek

MAROON
CREEK RD

TO
ASPEN

CRATER LAKE

Hike 16
Maroon - Snowmass Trail

Hiking distance: 3.8 miles round trip
Hiking time: 2.5 hours
Elevation gain: 400 feet
Topo: Trails Illustrated Maroon Bells/Redstone/Marble
U.S.G.S. Capitol Peak and Highland Peak

Summary of hike: The Maroon-Snowmass Trail follows Snowmass Creek upstream through a forest of aspens and evergreens. This trail offers beautiful views up the wooded canyon and spectacular views of the five surrounding mountain peaks.

Driving directions: There are two ways to the trailhead.
1) This route is shorter (13 miles), but the last two miles are steep and bumpy. From Aspen, drive 5 miles west on Highway 82 to Brush Creek Road on the left—turn left. Continue 5.2 miles to Divide Road on the right, 0.5 miles past Snowmass Village. Drive 0.9 miles on Divide Road to Base Lot E and the Krabloonik Restaurant. The road curves sharply to the left. Do not take the curve. Instead, continue straight onto an unpaved road, which descends 2.1 miles to the trailhead parking lot at the road end.
2) The longer route (25 miles) is smoother and scenic. Take Highway 82 west from Aspen for 13.5 miles to Snowmass Creek Road on the left—turn left. Continue up the valley 11 miles to a T-junction. Turn right and drive 0.5 miles to the trailhead parking lot at the road end.

Hiking directions: From the parking lot, pass through the metal gate. At 0.2 miles is a trail fork. Take the left fork, the "Maroon-Snowmass Trail." Continue upstream through the open expanse to a wooden gate. Pass through the gate to another trail fork, one mile from the trailhead. Take the left fork. Just past this junction you will see West Snowmass Creek cascading into Snowmass Creek. The trail leads to a second wooden gate. About 50 yards past the gate is a stream crossing at the Maroon Bells Wilderness border. This is the turnaround point. (The trail continues for an additional 15 miles.) To return, retrace your steps.

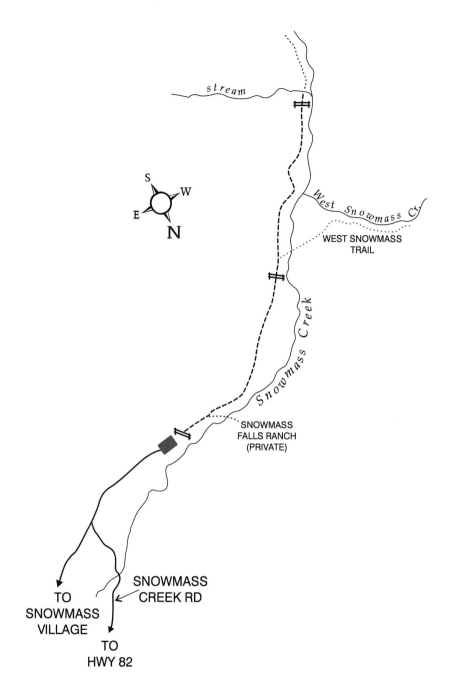

stream

West Snowmass Cr.

WEST SNOWMASS
TRAIL

Snowmass Creek

SNOWMASS
FALLS RANCH
(PRIVATE)

TO
SNOWMASS
VILLAGE

SNOWMASS
CREEK RD

TO
HWY 82

S W E N

MAROON-SNOWMASS TRAIL

NOTES

Information Sources

White River National Forest
Aspen Ranger District
806 W. Hallam
Aspen, CO 81611
(303) 925-3445

Aspen Chamber Resort Assoc.
425 Rio Grande Place
Aspen, CO 81611
(303) 925-1940
Fax: (303) 920-1173

Aspen Visitor Center
Wheeler Opera House
328 E. Hyman
Aspen, CO 81611
(303) 925-5656

Aspen Central Reservations
425 Rio Grande Place
Aspen, CO 81611
800-262-7736
(303) 925-9000

Aspen Historical Society
620 W. Bleeker
Aspen, CO 81611
(303) 925-3721

Basalt Chamber of Commerce
P.O. Box 514
Basalt, CO 81621
(303) 927-4031

Carbondale Chamber of Commerce
including Redstone and Marble
0590 Highway 133
Carbondale, CO 81623
(303) 963-1890

Snowmass Resort Association
P.O. Box 5566
Snowmass Village, CO 81615
(303) 923-2000

Aspen Center for Environmental
Studies at Hallam Lake
100 Puppy Smith Street
Aspen, CO 81611
(303) 925-5756

Roaring Fork Transit Agency (RFTA)
(303) 925-8484

Trail Conditions
U.S. Forest Service
(303) 920-1664

Other Day Hike Guidebooks

___ Day Hikes on Oahu $6.95
___ Day Hikes on Maui 6.95
___ Day Hikes on Kauai 6.95
___ Day Trips on St. Martin 9.95
___ Day Hikes in Denver 6.95
___ Day Hikes in Boulder, Colorado 6.95
___ Day Hikes in Steamboat Springs, Colorado 6.95
___ Day Hikes in Summit County, Colorado
    Breckenridge, Dillon, Frisco, Keystone, and Silverthorne 6.95
___ Day Hikes in Aspen, Colorado 7.95
___ Day Hikes in Yellowstone National Park
    25 Favorite Hikes 7.95
___ Day Hikes in the Grand Tetons and Jackson Hole 7.95
___ Day Hikes in Los Angeles
    Venice/Santa Monica to Topanga Canyon 6.95
___ Day Hikes in the Beartooths
    Red Lodge to Cooke City, Montana 4.95

These books may be purchased at your local bookstore or they will be glad to order them. For a full list of titles available directly from ICS Books, call toll-free 1-800-541-7323. Visa or Mastercard accepted.

Please include $2.00 per order to cover postage and handling.
Please send the books marked above. I enclose $ _____

Name _____

Address _____

City _____ State _____ Zip _____

Credit Card # _____ Exp. _____

Signature _____

1-800-541-7323

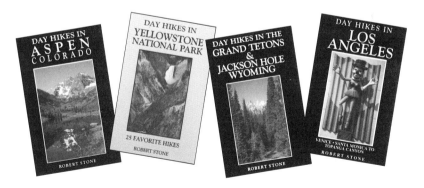

About the Author

The lure of the beautiful Rocky Mountains drew Robert to Red Lodge, Montana, in 1979. Hiking, exploring, and living in the Rockies has fulfilled a lifelong dream.

Robert Stone has traveled and photographed extensively throughout Asia, Europe, the Caribbean, Hawaii, and the Continental United States.